Jannay

Unit 8
Assessment

Level 1

Workbook

A Division of The McGraw-Hill Companies

Columbus, Ohio

www.sra4kids.com

SRA/McGraw-Hill
A Division of The **McGraw·Hill** Companies

2005 Imprint
Copyright © 2002 by SRA/McGraw-Hill.

All rights reserved. Except as permitted under the United States Copyright Act, no part of this publication may be reproduced or distributed in any form or by any means, or stored in a database or retrieval system, without the prior written permission of the publisher, unless otherwise indicated.

Send all inquiries to:
SRA/McGraw-Hill
8787 Orion Place
Columbus, OH 43240-4027

Printed in the United States of America.

ISBN 0-07-571338-1

9 MAZ 07 06

Table of Contents

Lesson Assessments

Lesson 2: A Game Called Piggle 2

Lesson 3: Jafta 6

Lesson 4: Mary Mack 10

Lesson 5: Matthew and Tilly 14

Lesson 6: The Great Ball Game 18

Lesson 7: The Big Team Relay Race 22

Lessons 1-8: Spelling Pretest and Final Tests 26

End of Unit Assessments

Multiple Choice Assessments

Comprehension Assessment 34

Spelling Assessment 36

Vocabulary Assessment 37

Grammar, Usage, and Mechanics Assessment 38

Writer's Craft Assessment 39

Teacher Directed Assessments

Oral Fluency Assessment 40

Listening Assessment 41

Writing Prompt 42

Name _____ Date _____ Score _____

UNIT 8 Games • Lesson 2

A Game Called Piggle

Read the following questions carefully. Then completely fill in the bubble of each correct answer. You may look back at the story to find the answer to each of the questions.

1. In this story, who asks Bear to play a game?
   - Ⓐ a fox
   - Ⓑ a puppy
   - ● a boy

2. When Homer first asks Bear to play, Bear says
   - Ⓐ yes
   - Ⓑ no
   - ● maybe

3. Homer wants to play
   - Ⓐ hide-and-seek
   - ● Piggle
   - Ⓒ ball

Read the following question carefully. Use a complete sentence to answer the question.

4. What happens after Bear starts singing?

   Baer sang Diddley widdley.

A Game Called Piggle (continued)

Read the following questions carefully. Then completely fill in the bubble of each correct answer.

5. What makes the game of Piggle sound nice?
   - Ⓐ the words have the same sounds
   - Ⓑ the words are all about animals
   - Ⓒ the words are in bear language

6. At the end of the story, Bear and Homer are
   - Ⓐ singing
   - Ⓑ shouting
   - Ⓒ laughing

Read the following question carefully. Use a complete sentence to answer the question.

7. Why does Bear say, "Give me time"?

   the boy Bear I no a game

Personal Response Write about a time you taught someone a game.

I play a hide-and seek

A Game Called Piggle (continued)

Vocabulary

Read the following questions carefully. Then completely fill in the bubble of each correct answer.

1. What is another word for **giggle**?
   - Ⓐ laugh
   - Ⓑ talk
   - Ⓒ move

2. A **game** is
   - Ⓐ something you build
   - Ⓑ something you find
   - Ⓒ something you play

3. What does it mean to **play** something?
   - Ⓐ to do it to get smart
   - Ⓑ to do it for fun
   - Ⓒ to do it just to win

4. When Homer says, **"Oh, I see,"** what does he mean?
   - Ⓐ "Oh, I understand."
   - Ⓑ "Oh, that's funny."
   - Ⓒ "Oh, I'm looking."

A Game Called Piggle (continued)

Phonics Review

Listen carefully. Then completely fill in the bubble of each correct answer.

1. Ⓐ bot   Ⓑ boat   Ⓒ bought
2. Ⓐ giggle   Ⓑ giggel   Ⓒ giggl
3. Ⓐ funne   Ⓑ funni   Ⓒ funny
4. Ⓐ thawt   Ⓑ thought   Ⓒ thot
5. Ⓐ little   Ⓑ littl   Ⓒ littel
6. Ⓐ nee   Ⓑ snee   Ⓒ knee
7. Ⓐ fot   Ⓑ fought   Ⓒ faut
8. Ⓐ ani   Ⓑ any   Ⓒ anee

Name _____ Date _____ Score _____

UNIT 8 Games • Lesson 3

Jafta

Read the following questions carefully. Then completely fill in the bubble of each correct answer. You may look back at the story to find the answer to each of the questions.

1. When Jafta is happy, he can skip like a
   - Ⓐ grasshopper
   - Ⓑ spider
   - Ⓒ water bug

2. Jafta can purr
   - Ⓐ like a kitten
   - Ⓑ like a cheetah
   - Ⓒ like a lion cub

3. Jafta wants to run as fast as
   - Ⓐ a cheetah and an eagle
   - Ⓑ a zebra and an ostrich
   - Ⓒ a cheetah and an ostrich

Read the following question carefully. Use a complete sentence to answer the question.

4. What is Jafta like when he is angry?

   _____

   _____

Jafta *(continued)*

Read the following questions carefully. Then completely fill in the bubble of each correct answer.

5. Jafta thinks it would be nicest of all to be a
   - Ⓐ giraffe
   - Ⓑ flamingo
   - Ⓒ lizard

6. Which of these is true about Jafta?
   - Ⓐ He is often angry.
   - Ⓑ He is usually happy.
   - Ⓒ He is always laughing.

Read the following question carefully. Use a complete sentence to answer the question.

7. Where do the flamingos fly in this story?

_____

_____

Personal Response Which animal would you most like to be? Why?

_____

_____

_____

_____

Jafta (continued)

Vocabulary

Read the following questions carefully. Then completely fill in the bubble of each correct answer.

1. An **impala** looks something like
   - Ⓐ a tiger
   - Ⓑ a pig
   - Ⓒ a deer

2. A **hyena** is like
   - Ⓐ a big bird
   - Ⓑ a small bug
   - Ⓒ a wild dog

3. To **nuzzle** means to
   - Ⓐ wiggle tails
   - Ⓑ rub your nose against something
   - Ⓒ roll over and over again

4. **Lazing** in the sun like a lizard means you are
   - Ⓐ eating
   - Ⓑ resting
   - Ⓒ chasing

5. When Jafta gets cross, he grumbles like a warthog. What is another word for **cross**?
   - Ⓐ angry
   - Ⓑ tired
   - Ⓒ sad

Jafta (continued)

Phonics Review

Fill in the bubble of the word that fits in the blank and is spelled correctly.

1. Do you _____ her name?
   Ⓐ know   Ⓑ now   Ⓒ gnow

2. Dad bought my mom a _____.
   Ⓐ rinj   Ⓑ rimg   Ⓒ ring

3. That is a bale of _____.
   Ⓐ stra   Ⓑ straw   Ⓒ strau

4. We were late _____ of snow.
   Ⓐ becaws   Ⓑ becas   Ⓒ because

5. Carol _____ her sister to school.
   Ⓐ brot   Ⓑ brought Ⓒ braut

6. Ms. Taft _____ us a new song.
   Ⓐ taught   Ⓑ tout   Ⓒ taght

Name _____ Date _____ Score _____

UNIT 8 Games • **Lesson 4**

Mary Mack

Read the following questions carefully. Then completely fill in the bubble of each correct answer. You may look back at the story to find the answer to each of the questions.

1. What color clothes does Mary wear?
   - Ⓐ purple
   - Ⓑ black
   - Ⓒ silver

2. How much money does Mary ask for?
   - Ⓐ fifty cents
   - Ⓑ forty cents
   - Ⓒ thirty cents

3. What does the elephant do?
   - Ⓐ It gives Mary a ride.
   - Ⓑ It jumps over a fence.
   - Ⓒ It eats peanuts.

Read the following question carefully. Use a complete sentence to answer the question.

4. When does the elephant come back?

_____

_____

Mary Mack *(continued)*

Read the following questions carefully. Then completely fill in the bubble of each correct answer.

5. Who gave Mary some money?
   - Ⓐ her mother
   - Ⓑ the elephant
   - Ⓒ Mack

6. How do you know this poem is make-believe?
   - Ⓐ because of Mary
   - Ⓑ because of the elephant
   - Ⓒ because of the buttons

Read the following question carefully. Use a complete sentence to answer the question.

7. Some words are said more than once in this story, such as <u>black</u>. How many times are these words said?

   _____

   _____

Personal Response What part of this story do you like best? Explain why.

   _____

   _____

   _____

Mary Mack (continued)

Vocabulary

Read the following questions carefully. Then completely fill in the bubble of each correct answer.

1. **High** means
   - Ⓐ tall
   - Ⓑ wide
   - Ⓒ small

2. In this story, a **button** is
   - Ⓐ something an elephant wears
   - Ⓑ another name for your nose
   - Ⓒ what keeps your clothes on

3. What is the **Fourth** of July?
   - Ⓐ a game
   - Ⓑ a holiday
   - Ⓒ an elephant

4. What does it mean to be **dressed** in something?
   - Ⓐ to wear something
   - Ⓑ to watch something
   - Ⓒ to learn something

Mary Mack *(continued)*

Phonics Review

Fill in the bubble of the word that fits in the blank and is spelled correctly.

1. Nan likes to _____ rope.
   - Ⓐ gump
   - Ⓑ chump
   - Ⓒ jump

2. Be sure to close the _____.
   - Ⓐ date
   - Ⓑ gate
   - Ⓒ pate

3. Did you _____ the letter?
   - Ⓐ rite
   - Ⓑ trite
   - Ⓒ write

4. The _____ is ringing.
   - Ⓐ phone
   - Ⓑ fone
   - Ⓒ pone

5. Dave hurt his _____.
   - Ⓐ led
   - Ⓑ leg
   - Ⓒ lej

6. Mr. Nance likes his _____.
   - Ⓐ gob
   - Ⓑ pob
   - Ⓒ job

Name _____ Date _____ Score _____

LESSON ASSESSMENT

UNIT 8 Games • **Lesson 5**

Matthew and Tilly

Read the following questions carefully. Then completely fill in the bubble of each correct answer. You may look back at the story to find the answer to each of the questions.

1. What brave thing did Matthew and Tilly do together?
   - Ⓐ They rescued a kitten from a tree.
   - Ⓑ They saved a kitten from a big dog.
   - Ⓒ They explored a cave.

2. What was Matthew and Tilly's reward?
   - Ⓐ a candy bar
   - Ⓑ money for ice cream
   - Ⓒ money for bubble gum

3. What does Tilly do after Matthew goes home?
   - Ⓐ rides her bike
   - Ⓑ makes lemonade
   - Ⓒ draws a sidewalk game

Read the following question carefully. Use a complete sentence to answer the question.

4. Why does Tilly get angry with Matthew?

_____

_____

Matthew and Tilly (*continued*)

Read the following questions carefully. Then completely fill in the bubble of each correct answer.

5. What do Matthew and Tilly learn in this story?
   - Ⓐ playing alone is much better
   - Ⓑ playing together is more fun
   - Ⓒ playing outside is best of all

6. What happens right before Matthew and Tilly start playing together again?
   - Ⓐ They say they are sorry.
   - Ⓑ They call each other names.
   - Ⓒ They wave at each other.

Read the following question carefully. Use a complete sentence to answer the question.

7. Why do Matthew and Tilly start playing together again?

_____

_____

Personal Response Write about a time when you made up with a friend.

_____

_____

_____

Unit 8 Assessment • *Matthew and Tilly* Unit 8 • Lesson 5

Matthew and Tilly (continued)

Vocabulary

Read the following questions carefully. Then completely fill in the bubble of each correct answer.

1. **Rescue** means
   - Ⓐ play
   - Ⓑ turn
   - Ⓒ save

2. The opposite of **brave** is
   - Ⓐ selfish
   - Ⓑ afraid
   - Ⓒ noisy

3. Sometimes Tilly and Matthew **got sick of** each other. What does this mean?
   - Ⓐ They got mad at each other.
   - Ⓑ They got in trouble together.
   - Ⓒ They got silly with each other.

4. What does a **crabby** voice sound like?
   - Ⓐ helpful
   - Ⓑ funny
   - Ⓒ angry

5. Matthew says that Tilly is **picky**. He thinks Tilly
   - Ⓐ is too sloppy
   - Ⓑ is too careful
   - Ⓒ is too bossy

Matthew and Tilly (continued)

Phonics Review

Listen carefully. Then completely fill in the bubble of each correct answer.

1. Ⓐ bake   Ⓑ bak   Ⓒ beak

2. Ⓐ rul   Ⓑ ruul   Ⓒ rule

3. Ⓐ fet   Ⓑ feet   Ⓒ feyt

4. Ⓐ tat   Ⓑ dhat   Ⓒ that

5. Ⓐ hid   Ⓑ hide   Ⓒ hiid

6. Ⓐ large   Ⓑ larj   Ⓒ larje

7. Ⓐ rod   Ⓑ road   Ⓒ roid

8. Ⓐ wid   Ⓑ wish   Ⓒ with

Name _____ Date _____ Score _____

UNIT 8 Games • Lesson 6

The Great Ball Game

Read the following questions carefully. Then completely fill in the bubble of each correct answer. You may look back at the story to find the answer to each of the questions.

1. Why did the Birds think they were better than the Animals?
   - Ⓐ The Birds had feathers.
   - Ⓑ The Birds had teeth.
   - Ⓒ The Birds had wings.

2. Who was the leader of the Animals?
   - Ⓐ Bear
   - Ⓑ Crane
   - Ⓒ Lion

3. What do the Birds and the Animals decide to do?
   - Ⓐ run in a race
   - Ⓑ play a ball game
   - Ⓒ make up a song

4. Why do the Animals decide to let Bat join their team?
   - Ⓐ Small animals can sometimes help.
   - Ⓑ Small animals have very large teeth.
   - Ⓒ Small animals always win games.

The Great Ball Game (continued)

Read the following question carefully. Use a complete sentence to answer the question.

5. Why didn't Bat know what team to play on?

_____

_____

Read the following question carefully. Then completely fill in the bubble of the correct answer.

6. According to the story, why does Bat fly after dark?
   - Ⓐ to see if the Animals need him to play ball
   - Ⓑ to see if the Birds are around
   - Ⓒ to look for the full moon

Read the following question carefully. Use a complete sentence to answer the question.

7. What does Bat help the Animals prove?

_____

_____

Personal Response What might have happened if no one had agreed to let Bat be on a team?

_____

_____

The Great Ball Game (continued)

Vocabulary

Read the following questions carefully. Then completely fill in the bubble of each correct answer.

1. An **argument** is like a
   - Ⓐ meal
   - Ⓑ party
   - Ⓒ fight

2. A **penalty** is like
   - Ⓐ a punishment
   - Ⓑ an award
   - Ⓒ a speech

3. To **prove** something, means to
   - Ⓐ find it by yourself
   - Ⓑ show that it is true
   - Ⓒ tell no one about it

4. **Creature** is another word for
   - Ⓐ animal
   - Ⓑ pet
   - Ⓒ cloud

5. Fox and deer say they are swift runners. **Swift** means
   - Ⓐ poor
   - Ⓑ slow
   - Ⓒ fast

The Great Ball Game (continued)

Phonics Review

Listen carefully. Then completely fill in the bubble of each correct answer.

1. Ⓐ bot   Ⓑ but   Ⓒ bat

2. Ⓐ red   Ⓑ rid   Ⓒ rad

3. Ⓐ muss   Ⓑ moss   Ⓒ miss

4. Ⓐ set   Ⓑ sut   Ⓒ sat

5. Ⓐ rick   Ⓑ rock   Ⓒ rack

6. Ⓐ men   Ⓑ mun   Ⓒ min

7. Ⓐ hed   Ⓑ hud   Ⓒ had

8. Ⓐ tep   Ⓑ top   Ⓒ tup

Name _____ Date _____ Score _____

UNIT 8 Games • Lesson 7

The Big Team Relay Race

Read the following questions carefully. Then completely fill in the bubble of each correct answer. You may look back at the story to find the answer to each of the questions.

1. Which animals are running in the beginning of this race?
    - Ⓐ Dog, Frog, and Owl
    - Ⓑ Dog, Frog, and Turtle
    - Ⓒ Dog, Frog, and Cat

2. Which relay racer does not have a stick?
    - Ⓐ Turtle
    - Ⓑ Frog
    - Ⓒ Dog

3. Who passes his stick to Rabbit?
    - Ⓐ Turtle
    - Ⓑ Frog
    - Ⓒ Dog

Read the following question carefully. Use a complete sentence to answer the question.

4. Which team wins the race?

_____

The Big Team Relay Race (continued)

Read the following questions carefully. Then completely fill in the bubble of each correct answer.

5. What does Dog carry for a stick?
   - Ⓐ a broom
   - Ⓑ a rope
   - Ⓒ a worm

6. Why doesn't Duck finish the race?
   - Ⓐ She is stuck in a mud puddle.
   - Ⓑ She hurts her big web feet.
   - Ⓒ She does not follow the rules.

Read the following question carefully. Use a complete sentence to answer the question.

7. Before Duck falls down, she is far, far ahead of Cat and Rabbit. How do you know this is true?

   _____

   _____

Personal Response Write about a time you have been in a race.

   _____

   _____

   _____

   _____

Unit 8 Assessment • *The Big Team Relay Race*   Unit 8 • Lesson 7

The Big Team Relay Race (continued)

Vocabulary

Read the following questions carefully. Then completely fill in the bubble of each correct answer.

1. In a **relay** race, each person
   - Ⓐ runs part of the way
   - Ⓑ has to run forward then backward
   - Ⓒ has to wiggle across the finish line

2. A **track** is where
   - Ⓐ animals are kept
   - Ⓑ races take place
   - Ⓒ birds are fed

3. **Wiggle** means almost the same as
   - Ⓐ shake
   - Ⓑ talk
   - Ⓒ laugh

4. To **cross** the finish line means to
   - Ⓐ get rid of it
   - Ⓑ be mad at it
   - Ⓒ go over it

5. **Zoom** is a sound that means
   - Ⓐ very happy
   - Ⓑ very fast
   - Ⓒ very quiet

Name _____ Date _____ Score _____

UNIT 8 Games • Lessons 7–8 *The Big Team Relay Race*

Spelling Final Test: Review Sound Spellings

Look at the underlined words. Find the one that is spelled wrong. Fill in its circle.

1. Ⓐ Can I eat lunch at your house?
   Ⓑ Mary had a little lam.
   Ⓒ We had a big storm last night.
   Ⓓ All the underlined words are spelled right.

2. Ⓕ Please stand in line at the door.
   Ⓖ Look at eech word.
   Ⓗ I like to eat pizza.
   Ⓙ All the underlined words are spelled right.

3. Ⓐ Use chalk to draw on the board.
   Ⓑ The line for lunch is long.
   Ⓒ My dog has bigg paws.
   Ⓓ All the underlined words are spelled right.

4. Ⓕ Write the words on the lin.
   Ⓖ The lamb was all white.
   Ⓗ The opposite of small is big.
   Ⓙ All the underlined words are spelled right.

5. Ⓐ You can drow a picture of your pet.
   Ⓑ Put a book on each desk.
   Ⓒ We eat lunch at noon.
   Ⓓ All the underlined words are spelled right.

Name _____ Date _____ Score _____

UNIT 8 Games

Comprehension Assessment

Read the following selection and questions carefully. Then completely fill in the bubble of each correct answer.

Luke Learns a New Game

"What's this, Uncle Nick?"

"It's a chessboard. The things on it are chessmen. I'm going to teach you how to play chess, Luke."

"I'm too little," said Luke. "Chess is for grownups." He frowned as he looked at his uncle.

"You are a smart boy, Luke. I think you'll like it. Each piece has a different name. Here's how they move."

Uncle Nick took his time. He named all the chess pieces. He showed Luke how they moved. Luke was still frowning, but he watched his uncle. Chess looked interesting. It might be fun.

"What are you two doing?" asked Kate. She was Luke's older sister. They were also best friends.

"We're playing chess." All of a sudden, Luke liked the game. Kate didn't know how to play chess. He wanted to do something she couldn't.

Kate made a face at Luke. Then she gave him a hug. "I love you, Lukie. I'm just teasing. You learn to play chess. Then you can teach me. It will be fun."

Luke said good-bye to Kate. Then he turned to Uncle Nick. "Okay, Uncle Nick. Teach me how to play chess."

Comprehension Assessment *(continued)*

1. What game does Uncle Nick want to teach Luke?
   - Ⓐ soccer
   - Ⓑ checkers
   - Ⓒ chess

2. Which character will learn to play chess last?
   - Ⓐ Kate
   - Ⓑ Luke
   - Ⓒ Uncle Nick

3. How did Kate tease Luke?
   - Ⓐ She gave him a hug.
   - Ⓑ She made a face at him.
   - Ⓒ She told him she wanted to learn chess.

Read the following questions carefully. Answer each question with a complete sentence.

4. Why doesn't Luke think he can learn to play chess?

   _____

   _____

5. What is the main reason Luke wants to learn to play chess?

   _____

   _____

Unit 8 Assessment • *Comprehension Assessment*

Name _____ Date _____ Score _____

UNIT 8 Games

Spelling Assessment

Look at the underlined words. Find the one that is spelled wrong. Fill in its circle.

1. Ⓐ We rode on a donkey at the zoo.
   Ⓑ I can hear the phone ringing.
   Ⓒ The purpel grapes are sour.
   Ⓓ We ran home from school.

2. Ⓕ I know how to spell my name.
   Ⓖ My dog has a thorn in its pau.
   Ⓗ James lives in that home.
   Ⓙ I saw the moon last night.

3. Ⓐ I can jump off the high diving board.
   Ⓑ A lamb is a baby sheep.
   Ⓒ We like to swing on the monkey bars.
   Ⓓ I don't like to eet carrots.

4. Ⓕ We ran all the way to school.
   Ⓖ My age is six.
   Ⓗ I'd like to meet your famuly.
   Ⓙ I rode on a train.

5. Ⓐ Hens sit on their eggs.
   Ⓑ I saw a clown at the circus.
   Ⓒ Would you like to learn how to draw?
   Ⓓ I need a bij tube of toothpaste.

Name _____ Date _____ Score _____

UNIT 8 Games

Vocabulary Assessment

Look at the underlined word in each question. Then choose the answer that is closest in meaning to the underlined word.

SAMPLE

A <u>silent</u> person is a person who is—
- Ⓐ nice
- ● quiet
- Ⓒ angry
- Ⓓ hurt

1. <u>Yes</u> means—
   - Ⓐ okay
   - Ⓑ true
   - Ⓒ no
   - Ⓓ maybe

2. Something that is <u>high</u> is—
   - Ⓕ wet
   - Ⓖ a coin
   - Ⓗ like a sharp hill
   - Ⓙ tall

3. A <u>laugh</u> is a—
   - Ⓐ giggle
   - Ⓑ look
   - Ⓒ smile
   - Ⓓ nod

4. <u>Jump</u> means the same thing as—
   - Ⓕ dance
   - Ⓖ stroll
   - Ⓗ hop
   - Ⓙ walk

5. Something that is <u>big</u> is—
   - Ⓐ small
   - Ⓑ medium
   - Ⓒ hot
   - Ⓓ large

END OF UNIT ASSESSMENT
Multiple Choice

Unit 8 Assessment • *Vocabulary Assessment*   **37**

Name _____ Date _____ Score _____

UNIT 8 Games

Language: Grammar, Usage, and Mechanics Assessment

Choose the end mark that goes with each sentence.

1. Where are you going
    - Ⓐ .
    - Ⓑ ?
    - Ⓒ !

2. I'm going bird watching
    - Ⓕ .
    - Ⓖ ?
    - Ⓗ !

Choose the sentence part that is underlined.

3. The tall tree <u>fell in the storm</u>.
    - Ⓐ naming part
    - Ⓑ action part

4. The <u>tiny chipmunks</u> ran down the hole.
    - Ⓕ naming part
    - Ⓖ action part

Fill in the circle next to the correct contraction.

5. <u>He is</u> my friend.
    - Ⓐ He'd
    - Ⓑ She's
    - Ⓒ He's

Name _____ Date _____ Score _____

UNIT 8 Games

Language: Writer's Craft Assessment

Fill in the circle next to the word that would be a good sensory detail to fill in the blank.

1. The blue jay's ___ chirping scared the other birds.
   - Ⓐ warm
   - Ⓑ bumpy
   - Ⓒ loud

2. The bird pecked to break the ___ seed.
   - Ⓕ hard
   - Ⓖ loud
   - Ⓗ hairy

Fill in the circle next to the word that begins with a repeating sound.

3. Rabbits ___ and romp over rocks.
   - Ⓐ hop
   - Ⓑ jump
   - Ⓒ run

Choose the sentence that should be first in the paragraph.

4. It is open at the top. It is flat at the bottom. You can use a cup to drink milk or juice. It would be hard to drink without a cup.
   - Ⓕ A cup is made to be useful.
   - Ⓖ Some cups have handles.
   - Ⓗ I like to drink apple juice.
   - Ⓙ We have lots of dishes.

Name _____ Date _____ Score _____

END OF UNIT ASSESSMENT — Teacher-Directed

UNIT 8 Games

Oral Fluency Assessment

A Game of Tag

It was a warm day. The sun was shining. Dot was playing outside. She saw her friend, Ken.

"Do you want to play tag?" asked Dot. Ken said he did. They looked for more friends. That way the game would be more fun.

They went to Pat's house. She said she would play. Her brother, Mark, wanted to play, too.

The four children went to Dot's yard. They were all set to play. Then Ken's dog, Brownie, ran into the yard. The children laughed. Brownie wanted to play tag with them, too.

Name _____ Date _____ Score _____

UNIT 8 Games

Listening Assessment

Listen carefully to each question as it is read to you. Then answer the questions below.

1. Ⓐ a bag
   Ⓑ a box
   Ⓒ a backpack
   Ⓓ a jar

2. Ⓕ a model airplane set
   Ⓖ legos
   Ⓗ a model train set
   Ⓙ a wooden block set

3. Ⓐ roll it
   Ⓑ bounce it
   Ⓒ throw it
   Ⓓ catch it

4. Ⓕ gym
   Ⓖ playground
   Ⓗ school
   Ⓙ park

5. Ⓐ a hat
   Ⓑ a helmet
   Ⓒ a glove
   Ⓓ a mask

6. Ⓕ play with a ball
   Ⓖ play hide and seek
   Ⓗ play on the swing
   Ⓙ talk on the phone

END OF UNIT ASSESSMENT Teacher-Directed

Name _____ Date _____ Score _____

END OF UNIT ASSESSMENT — Teacher-Directed

UNIT 8 Games

Expository Writing Prompt

Writing Situation
Everyone has a favorite toy.

Audience: Your classmates

Directions for Writing
Think about one of your favorite toys. Then tell why that one toy is your favorite.

Checklist
You will score the most points if you
- Name your topic in a sentence.
- Tell details about your topic.
- Stay on the topic.
- Use words to tell how you feel.
- Use words that describe.
- Write complete sentences.
- Use correct spelling, capital letters, end marks, and exact words.